50 Japanese Kitchen Recipes

By: Kelly Johnson

Table of Contents

- Miso Soup
- Tonkotsu Ramen
- Shoyu Ramen
- Miso Ramen
- Onigiri (Rice Balls)
- Tamago Kake Gohan (Egg Over Rice)
- Gyudon (Beef Bowl)
- Oyakodon (Chicken & Egg Bowl)
- Katsudon (Pork Cutlet Bowl)
- Unadon (Grilled Eel Bowl)
- Takikomi Gohan (Seasoned Rice)
- Sushi Rolls (Maki)
- Nigiri Sushi
- Temaki (Hand Rolls)
- Chirashi Sushi (Scattered Sushi)
- Soba Noodles (Cold or Hot)
- Udon Noodles (Kake Udon)
- Yaki Udon (Stir-Fried Udon)
- Hiyashi Chuka (Cold Ramen Salad)
- Zaru Soba (Chilled Soba with Dipping Sauce)
- Okonomiyaki (Savory Pancake)
- Takoyaki (Octopus Balls)
- Yakisoba (Stir-Fried Noodles)
- Tempura (Battered & Fried Seafood/Veggies)
- Karaage (Japanese Fried Chicken)
- Teriyaki Chicken
- Teriyaki Salmon
- Shogayaki (Ginger Pork)
- Gyoza (Japanese Dumplings)
- Chawanmushi (Savory Egg Custard)
- Nikujaga (Meat & Potato Stew)
- Japanese Curry Rice
- Katsu Curry (Curry with Fried Cutlet)
- Nabe (Hot Pot)
- Sukiyaki (Beef Hot Pot)

- Shabu-Shabu (Japanese Fondue)
- Tonkatsu (Breaded Pork Cutlet)
- Hambagu (Japanese Hamburger Steak)
- Omurice (Omelet Rice)
- Tamagoyaki (Rolled Omelet)
- Dashimaki Tamago (Broth-Flavored Omelet)
- Hiyayakko (Chilled Tofu with Toppings)
- Agedashi Tofu (Fried Tofu in Broth)
- Tsukemono (Japanese Pickles)
- Edamame (Boiled Soybeans)
- Anmitsu (Sweet Jelly Dessert)
- Dorayaki (Red Bean Pancakes)
- Mochi (Rice Cake)
- Taiyaki (Fish-Shaped Pastry)
- Matcha Ice Cream

Miso Soup

Ingredients:

- 4 cups dashi (Japanese soup stock)
- 3 tbsp miso paste
- ½ cup tofu (cubed)
- 1 tbsp wakame (dried seaweed)
- 2 green onions (sliced)

Instructions:

1. Heat dashi in a pot over medium heat until warm (do not boil).
2. Dissolve miso paste in a small amount of dashi, then stir into the pot.
3. Add tofu and wakame, cook for 2 minutes.
4. Garnish with green onions and serve.

Tonkotsu Ramen

Ingredients:

- 4 cups pork bone broth
- 2 servings ramen noodles
- 2 slices chashu pork
- 1 soft-boiled egg (halved)
- 1 tbsp soy sauce
- 2 green onions (sliced)
- 1 sheet nori (seaweed)

Instructions:

1. Cook ramen noodles according to package instructions.
2. Heat pork bone broth and soy sauce in a pot.
3. Divide cooked noodles into bowls, pour broth over them.
4. Top with chashu, egg, green onions, and nori.

Shoyu Ramen

Ingredients:

- 4 cups chicken broth
- 2 tbsp soy sauce
- 1 tbsp mirin
- 2 servings ramen noodles
- 2 slices chashu pork
- 1 soft-boiled egg (halved)
- 2 green onions (sliced)

Instructions:

1. Cook ramen noodles and set aside.
2. Heat broth with soy sauce and mirin in a pot.
3. Pour broth over noodles in bowls.
4. Add toppings and serve.

Miso Ramen

Ingredients:

- 4 cups chicken or pork broth
- 2 tbsp miso paste
- 2 servings ramen noodles
- 1 tbsp soy sauce
- 1 soft-boiled egg (halved)
- 2 green onions (sliced)
- 1 sheet nori

Instructions:

1. Cook ramen noodles and set aside.
2. Heat broth and dissolve miso paste.
3. Pour broth over noodles in bowls.
4. Add toppings and serve.

Onigiri (Rice Balls)

Ingredients:

- 2 cups cooked Japanese rice
- ½ tsp salt
- ½ cup filling (tuna mayo, salmon, pickled plum)
- 1 sheet nori (cut into strips)

Instructions:

1. Wet hands, sprinkle with salt, and shape rice around filling.
2. Form into a triangle or ball shape.
3. Wrap with nori and serve.

Tamago Kake Gohan (Egg Over Rice)

Ingredients:

- 1 cup hot cooked rice
- 1 raw egg
- 1 tsp soy sauce

Instructions:

1. Crack the egg into a bowl of hot rice.
2. Drizzle with soy sauce and mix well.

Gyudon (Beef Bowl)

Ingredients:

- 1 cup cooked rice
- ½ lb thinly sliced beef
- ½ onion (sliced)
- 2 tbsp soy sauce
- 1 tbsp mirin
- 1 tbsp sugar
- ½ cup dashi

Instructions:

1. Cook onion in dashi, soy sauce, mirin, and sugar.
2. Add beef and simmer until cooked.
3. Serve over rice.

Oyakodon (Chicken & Egg Bowl)

Ingredients:

- 1 cup cooked rice
- ½ lb chicken (cubed)
- ½ onion (sliced)
- 2 eggs (beaten)
- 2 tbsp soy sauce
- 1 tbsp mirin
- ½ cup dashi

Instructions:

1. Cook onion and chicken in dashi, soy sauce, and mirin.
2. Pour beaten eggs over and cover until set.
3. Serve over rice.

Katsudon (Pork Cutlet Bowl)

Ingredients:

- 1 cup cooked rice
- 1 pork cutlet (tonkatsu)
- ½ onion (sliced)
- 2 eggs (beaten)
- 2 tbsp soy sauce
- 1 tbsp mirin
- ½ cup dashi

Instructions:

1. Cook onion in dashi, soy sauce, and mirin.
2. Place sliced tonkatsu on top, pour eggs over, cover until set.
3. Serve over rice.

Unadon (Grilled Eel Bowl)

Ingredients:

- 1 cup cooked rice
- 1 grilled eel fillet (unagi)
- 2 tbsp unagi sauce

Instructions:

1. Heat grilled eel in a pan with unagi sauce.
2. Serve over rice.

Takikomi Gohan (Seasoned Rice)

Ingredients:

- 2 cups uncooked rice
- 2½ cups dashi
- 2 tbsp soy sauce
- 1 tbsp mirin
- ½ cup sliced mushrooms
- ½ cup diced carrots

Instructions:

1. Rinse rice and place in a rice cooker.
2. Add dashi, soy sauce, mirin, mushrooms, and carrots.
3. Cook as usual and serve.

Sushi Rolls (Maki)

Ingredients:

- 2 cups sushi rice (cooked & seasoned)
- 4 sheets nori (seaweed)
- ½ cup fillings (cucumber, avocado, crab, tuna, salmon)
- 1 tbsp rice vinegar
- Soy sauce, wasabi, and pickled ginger (for serving)

Instructions:

1. Place a sheet of nori on a bamboo mat, shiny side down.
2. Spread an even layer of rice, leaving 1 inch at the top.
3. Add fillings in a line near the bottom.
4. Roll tightly using the mat, sealing the edge with rice vinegar.
5. Slice into bite-sized pieces and serve.

Nigiri Sushi

Ingredients:

- 2 cups sushi rice (cooked & seasoned)
- 8 slices fresh fish (salmon, tuna, shrimp)
- 1 tsp wasabi

Instructions:

1. Wet hands and shape small rice balls.
2. Spread a little wasabi on each slice of fish.
3. Press the fish onto the rice and serve.

Temaki (Hand Rolls)

Ingredients:

- 2 cups sushi rice (cooked & seasoned)
- 4 sheets nori (cut in half)
- ½ cup fillings (tuna, avocado, cucumber, crab)

Instructions:

1. Place a nori sheet in your palm, shiny side down.
2. Spread rice on one side, leaving space at the edges.
3. Add fillings and roll into a cone shape.
4. Serve immediately.

Chirashi Sushi (Scattered Sushi)

Ingredients:

- 2 cups sushi rice (cooked & seasoned)
- ½ cup assorted sashimi (salmon, tuna, shrimp)
- ¼ cup sliced cucumber
- ¼ cup sliced avocado
- 1 tbsp tobiko (fish roe)

Instructions:

1. Spread sushi rice in a bowl.
2. Arrange sashimi, cucumber, avocado, and tobiko on top.
3. Serve with soy sauce and wasabi.

Soba Noodles (Cold or Hot)

Ingredients:

- 2 servings soba noodles
- 2 cups dashi (for hot version)
- 2 tbsp soy sauce
- 1 tbsp mirin
- Green onions and sesame seeds (for garnish)

Instructions:

1. Cook soba noodles, then rinse under cold water.
2. For hot: Serve in warm dashi broth.
3. For cold: Serve with dipping sauce (soy sauce, mirin, dashi).

Udon Noodles (Kake Udon)

Ingredients:

- 2 servings udon noodles
- 3 cups dashi
- 2 tbsp soy sauce
- 1 tbsp mirin
- Green onions and tempura flakes (for garnish)

Instructions:

1. Heat dashi with soy sauce and mirin.
2. Cook udon noodles separately.
3. Serve noodles in broth, topped with green onions.

Yaki Udon (Stir-Fried Udon)

Ingredients:

- 2 servings udon noodles
- ½ cup sliced vegetables (carrots, cabbage, mushrooms)
- ½ cup protein (chicken, shrimp, tofu)
- 2 tbsp soy sauce
- 1 tbsp sesame oil

Instructions:

1. Cook udon noodles and set aside.
2. Stir-fry vegetables and protein in sesame oil.
3. Add noodles and soy sauce, stir-fry for 2 minutes.

Hiyashi Chuka (Cold Ramen Salad)

Ingredients:

- 2 servings ramen noodles (cooked & cooled)
- ½ cup sliced cucumber
- ½ cup shredded chicken or ham
- 1 egg (thin omelet, sliced)
- 2 tbsp soy sauce
- 1 tbsp rice vinegar
- 1 tsp sesame oil

Instructions:

1. Mix soy sauce, vinegar, and sesame oil for dressing.
2. Arrange noodles with toppings in a bowl.
3. Drizzle with dressing and serve cold.

Zaru Soba (Chilled Soba with Dipping Sauce)

Ingredients:

- 2 servings soba noodles
- ½ cup mentsuyu (soba dipping sauce)
- 1 tbsp green onions (chopped)
- 1 tsp wasabi

Instructions:

1. Cook soba noodles, rinse under cold water, and drain.
2. Serve on a plate with mentsuyu sauce on the side.
3. Dip noodles in sauce before eating.

Okonomiyaki (Savory Pancake)

Ingredients:

- 1 cup flour
- ½ cup dashi or water
- 1 egg
- 1 cup shredded cabbage
- ½ cup protein (shrimp, pork, or bacon)
- 2 tbsp okonomiyaki sauce
- 1 tbsp mayonnaise
- Bonito flakes and green onions for topping

Instructions:

1. Mix flour, dashi, and egg into a batter.
2. Stir in cabbage and protein.
3. Cook on a greased pan for 4 minutes per side.
4. Top with sauce, mayo, and bonito flakes.

Takoyaki (Octopus Balls)

Ingredients:

- 1 cup takoyaki batter (flour, dashi, egg)
- ½ cup diced octopus
- ¼ cup green onions (chopped)
- ¼ cup tempura flakes
- 2 tbsp takoyaki sauce
- 1 tbsp mayonnaise
- Bonito flakes for topping

Instructions:

1. Heat a takoyaki pan and grease it.
2. Pour batter into molds, add octopus, green onions, and tempura flakes.
3. Cook, turning with a skewer until golden brown.
4. Drizzle with sauce, mayo, and bonito flakes.

Yakisoba (Stir-Fried Noodles)

Ingredients:

- 2 servings yakisoba noodles
- ½ cup sliced cabbage
- ½ cup sliced carrots
- ½ cup sliced pork or chicken
- 2 tbsp yakisoba sauce
- 1 tbsp oil
- Green onions and bonito flakes for garnish

Instructions:

1. Heat oil in a pan, cook meat until browned.
2. Add vegetables and stir-fry until tender.
3. Add noodles and yakisoba sauce, stir-fry for 2 minutes.
4. Garnish and serve.

Tempura (Battered & Fried Seafood/Veggies)

Ingredients:

- ½ cup shrimp, sweet potatoes, or bell peppers
- ½ cup flour
- ½ cup ice-cold water
- 1 egg
- Oil for frying

Instructions:

1. Mix flour, egg, and ice-cold water to form a light batter.
2. Dip ingredients into batter and fry in hot oil until golden brown.
3. Drain and serve with tempura dipping sauce.

Karaage (Japanese Fried Chicken)

Ingredients:

- ½ lb chicken thighs (cut into bite-sized pieces)
- 2 tbsp soy sauce
- 1 tbsp sake
- 1 tsp grated ginger
- ½ cup potato starch
- Oil for frying

Instructions:

1. Marinate chicken in soy sauce, sake, and ginger for 15 minutes.
2. Coat with potato starch and deep-fry until golden and crispy.
3. Drain and serve with lemon wedges.

Teriyaki Chicken

Ingredients:

- 2 chicken thighs
- 2 tbsp soy sauce
- 1 tbsp mirin
- 1 tbsp sugar
- 1 tbsp sake

Instructions:

1. Cook chicken in a pan until golden brown.
2. Add soy sauce, mirin, sugar, and sake.
3. Simmer until sauce thickens, then serve.

Teriyaki Salmon

Ingredients:

- 2 salmon fillets
- 2 tbsp soy sauce
- 1 tbsp mirin
- 1 tbsp sugar
- 1 tbsp sake

Instructions:

1. Cook salmon in a pan until golden.
2. Add soy sauce, mirin, sugar, and sake.
3. Simmer until sauce thickens, then serve.

Shogayaki (Ginger Pork)

Ingredients:

- ½ lb thinly sliced pork
- 2 tbsp soy sauce
- 1 tbsp sake
- 1 tbsp mirin
- 1 tbsp grated ginger

Instructions:

1. Cook pork in a pan until browned.
2. Add soy sauce, sake, mirin, and ginger.
3. Simmer for a minute and serve.

Gyoza (Japanese Dumplings)

Ingredients:

- 20 gyoza wrappers
- ½ lb ground pork
- ½ cup cabbage (chopped)
- 1 clove garlic (minced)
- 1 tsp soy sauce
- 1 tsp sesame oil

Instructions:

1. Mix pork, cabbage, garlic, soy sauce, and sesame oil.
2. Place a spoonful of filling in each wrapper, fold, and seal.
3. Pan-fry until crispy, then add water and steam for 3 minutes.

Chawanmushi (Savory Egg Custard)

Ingredients:

- 2 eggs
- 1 cup dashi
- 1 tsp soy sauce
- ½ tsp mirin
- ½ cup fillings (shrimp, mushroom, fish cake)

Instructions:

1. Whisk eggs with dashi, soy sauce, and mirin.
2. Pour into cups with fillings.
3. Steam for 10 minutes until set.

Nikujaga (Meat & Potato Stew)

Ingredients:

- ½ lb beef (thinly sliced)
- 2 potatoes (cubed)
- ½ onion (sliced)
- 2 tbsp soy sauce
- 1 tbsp sugar
- 1 cup dashi

Instructions:

1. Cook beef and onions in a pot.
2. Add potatoes, soy sauce, sugar, and dashi.
3. Simmer until potatoes are tender.

Japanese Curry Rice

Ingredients:

- ½ lb beef or chicken (cubed)
- 2 potatoes (cubed)
- 1 carrot (sliced)
- ½ onion (chopped)
- 2 cups water
- 1 block Japanese curry roux

Instructions:

1. Cook meat, onion, and carrots in a pot.
2. Add potatoes and water, simmer until tender.
3. Stir in curry roux until dissolved, then serve over rice.

Katsu Curry (Curry with Fried Cutlet)

Ingredients:

- 1 tonkatsu (fried pork cutlet)
- 1 serving Japanese curry (see recipe above)
- 1 cup cooked rice

Instructions:

1. Prepare Japanese curry.
2. Slice tonkatsu and place on top of rice.
3. Pour curry over and serve.

Nabe (Hot Pot)

Ingredients:

- 4 cups dashi broth
- ½ lb sliced chicken, pork, or seafood
- ½ block tofu (cubed)
- 1 cup Napa cabbage (chopped)
- ½ cup shiitake mushrooms
- ½ cup carrots (sliced)
- ½ cup udon noodles (optional)

Instructions:

1. Bring dashi broth to a simmer in a pot.
2. Add meat, tofu, and vegetables, cooking until tender.
3. Add noodles if desired, and serve with dipping sauces.

Sukiyaki (Beef Hot Pot)

Ingredients:

- ½ lb thinly sliced beef
- 2 cups dashi
- 2 tbsp soy sauce
- 1 tbsp mirin
- 1 tbsp sugar
- ½ block tofu (cubed)
- 1 cup Napa cabbage (chopped)
- ½ cup mushrooms
- 1 raw egg (for dipping)

Instructions:

1. Heat dashi, soy sauce, mirin, and sugar in a pot.
2. Add beef, tofu, and vegetables, cooking until tender.
3. Dip cooked ingredients into raw egg before eating.

Shabu-Shabu (Japanese Fondue)

Ingredients:

- ½ lb thinly sliced beef or pork
- 4 cups dashi broth
- 1 cup Napa cabbage (chopped)
- ½ cup mushrooms
- ½ block tofu (cubed)
- 1 cup udon noodles

Instructions:

1. Heat dashi broth to a simmer.
2. Swish thin slices of meat in the broth until cooked.
3. Add vegetables and tofu, cooking until tender.
4. Serve with ponzu or sesame dipping sauce.

Tonkatsu (Breaded Pork Cutlet)

Ingredients:

- 2 pork cutlets
- ½ cup flour
- 1 egg (beaten)
- ½ cup panko breadcrumbs
- Oil for frying

Instructions:

1. Coat pork in flour, dip in egg, then coat with panko.
2. Fry in hot oil until golden brown.
3. Drain and serve with tonkatsu sauce.

Hambagu (Japanese Hamburger Steak)

Ingredients:

- ½ lb ground beef
- ¼ cup panko breadcrumbs
- 1 egg
- 1 tbsp milk
- 1 tbsp soy sauce
- ½ onion (chopped)

Instructions:

1. Mix all ingredients and shape into patties.
2. Cook in a pan until browned and cooked through.
3. Serve with demi-glace sauce or ketchup.

Omurice (Omelet Rice)

Ingredients:

- 1 cup cooked rice
- ½ cup chicken (diced)
- 2 tbsp ketchup
- 2 eggs
- 1 tbsp butter

Instructions:

1. Sauté chicken and rice, add ketchup, and mix well.
2. Beat eggs and cook into an omelet.
3. Place the omelet over rice and serve with extra ketchup.

Tamagoyaki (Rolled Omelet)

Ingredients:

- 2 eggs
- 1 tbsp sugar
- 1 tsp soy sauce
- 1 tsp dashi

Instructions:

1. Beat eggs with sugar, soy sauce, and dashi.
2. Cook in a pan, rolling layers as you go.
3. Slice and serve.

Dashimaki Tamago (Broth-Flavored Omelet)

Ingredients:

- 2 eggs
- 2 tbsp dashi
- 1 tsp soy sauce

Instructions:

1. Beat eggs with dashi and soy sauce.
2. Cook in a pan, rolling layers as you go.
3. Slice and serve warm.

Hiyayakko (Chilled Tofu with Toppings)

Ingredients:

- ½ block silken tofu
- 1 tbsp soy sauce
- 1 tbsp green onions (chopped)
- 1 tsp grated ginger

Instructions:

1. Place tofu on a plate.
2. Top with soy sauce, green onions, and ginger.
3. Serve chilled.

Agedashi Tofu (Fried Tofu in Broth)

Ingredients:

- ½ block firm tofu
- ¼ cup potato starch
- Oil for frying
- ½ cup dashi broth
- 1 tbsp soy sauce
- 1 tsp mirin

Instructions:

1. Coat tofu cubes in potato starch and fry until golden.
2. Heat dashi, soy sauce, and mirin.
3. Pour broth over tofu and serve.

Tsukemono (Japanese Pickles)

Ingredients:

- ½ cucumber (sliced)
- ½ cup daikon radish (sliced)
- 1 tbsp salt
- 1 tbsp rice vinegar

Instructions:

1. Mix vegetables with salt and let sit for 30 minutes.
2. Rinse and mix with rice vinegar.
3. Chill before serving.

Edamame (Boiled Soybeans)

Ingredients:

- 1 cup fresh or frozen edamame (soybeans)
- 1 tsp salt
- Water for boiling

Instructions:

1. Boil water in a pot and add salt.
2. Add edamame and cook for 3-5 minutes.
3. Drain and sprinkle with extra salt before serving.

Anmitsu (Sweet Jelly Dessert)

Ingredients:

- 1 cup kanten (agar) jelly, cubed
- ½ cup sweet red bean paste (anko)
- ½ cup fresh fruit (strawberries, kiwi, or oranges)
- ¼ cup mochi pieces (optional)
- ½ cup kuromitsu (black sugar syrup)

Instructions:

1. Arrange kanten jelly cubes, fruit, and mochi in a bowl.
2. Top with sweet red bean paste.
3. Drizzle with kuromitsu syrup before serving.

Dorayaki (Red Bean Pancakes)

Ingredients:

- 1 cup flour
- 2 eggs
- 2 tbsp sugar
- ½ cup milk
- 1 tsp baking powder
- ½ cup sweet red bean paste

Instructions:

1. Mix flour, eggs, sugar, milk, and baking powder to form a batter.
2. Cook small pancakes on a pan until golden brown.
3. Spread red bean paste on one pancake and sandwich with another.

Mochi (Rice Cake)

Ingredients:

- 1 cup glutinous rice flour
- ½ cup water
- ¼ cup sugar
- Cornstarch for dusting

Instructions:

1. Mix rice flour, water, and sugar in a bowl.
2. Microwave for 2 minutes, stir, and heat for another minute.
3. Dust surface with cornstarch, shape the mochi, and let cool before serving.

Taiyaki (Fish-Shaped Pastry)

Ingredients:

- 1 cup flour
- ½ tsp baking powder
- 1 egg
- ½ cup milk
- ¼ cup sugar
- ½ cup sweet red bean paste

Instructions:

1. Mix flour, baking powder, egg, milk, and sugar to form a batter.
2. Pour batter into a taiyaki mold, add red bean paste, and cover with more batter.
3. Cook until golden brown on both sides.

Matcha Ice Cream

Ingredients:

- 1 cup heavy cream
- ½ cup milk
- 2 tbsp matcha powder
- ¼ cup sugar

Instructions:

1. Whisk matcha powder with milk until dissolved.
2. Add heavy cream and sugar, mixing well.
3. Freeze for 4-6 hours, stirring occasionally.

www.ingramcontent.com/pod-product-compliance
Lightning Source LLC
LaVergne TN
LVHW081340060526
838201LV00055B/2761